Understanding the Films of

SPIKE
LEE

by Mike Reynolds

ABDO
Publishing Company

Essential Critiques

How to Analyze the Films of

SPIKE LEE

by Mike Reynolds

Content Consultant: Keith M. Harris, associate professor
Department of Media and Cultural Studies, University of California, Riverside

Credits

Published by ABDO Publishing Company, 8000 West 78th Street, Edina, Minnesota 55439. Copyright © 2011 by Abdo Consulting Group, Inc. International copyrights reserved in all countries. No part of this book may be reproduced in any form without written permission from the publisher. The Essential Library™ is a trademark and logo of ABDO Publishing Company.

Printed in the United States of America,
North Mankato, Minnesota
062010
092010

 THIS BOOK CONTAINS AT LEAST 10% RECYCLED MATERIALS.

Editors: Rebecca Rowell, Nadia Higgins, and Mari Kesselring
Copy Editor: David Johnstone
Interior Design and Production: Marie Tupy
Cover Design: Marie Tupy

Library of Congress Cataloging-in-Publication Data
Reynolds, Mike.
  How to analyze the films of Spike Lee / Mike Reynolds.
      p. cm. — (Essential critiques)
  Includes bibliographical references and index.
  ISBN 978-1-61613-530-0
1. Lee, Spike—Criticism and interpretation. 2. Film criticism—Juvenile
literature. I. Title.
  PN1998.3.L44R49 2010
  791.4302'33092—dc22

                                         2010015754

Table of Contents

1

Introduction to Critiques

What Is Critical Theory?

What do you usually do as a member of an audience watching a movie? You probably enjoy the settings, the costumes, and the sound track. You learn about the characters as they are developed through dialogue and other interactions. You might be drawn in by the plot of the movie, eager to find out what happens next. Yet these are only a few of many ways of understanding and appreciating a movie. What if you are interested in delving more deeply? You might want to learn more about the director and how his or her personal background is reflected in the film. Or you might want to examine what the film says about society—how it depicts the roles of women and minorities, for example. If so, you have entered the realm of critical theory.

Critical theory helps you learn how various
works of art, literature, music, theater, film, and
other endeavors either support or challenge the way
society behaves. Critical theory is the evaluation
and interpretation of a work using different
philosophies, or schools of thought. Critical theory
can be used to understand all types of cultural
productions.

There are many different critical theories. If
you are analyzing a movie, each theory asks you
to look at the work from a different perspective.
Some theories address social issues, while others
focus on the director's life, what role the direction
plays in the overall film, or the time period in
which the film was written or set. For example, the

critical theory that asks how a director's life and filmmaking style affected the work is called auteur criticism. Other common, broad schools of criticism include historical criticism, feminist criticism, and ideological criticism.

What Is the Purpose of Critical Theory?

Critical theory can open your mind to new ways of thinking. It can help you evaluate a movie from a new perspective, directing your attention to issues and messages you may not otherwise recognize in a work. For example, applying feminist criticism to a film may make you aware of female stereotypes perpetuated in the work. Applying a critical theory to a work helps you learn about the person who created it or the society that enjoyed it. You can explore how the movie is perceived by current cultures.

How Do You Apply Critical Theory?

You conduct a critique when you use a critical theory to examine and question a work. The theory you choose is a lens through which you can view the work, or a springboard for asking questions about the work. Applying a critical theory helps you to think critically about the work. You are free to question the work and make an assertion about it. If you choose to examine a film using auteur theory, for example, you want to know how the director's personal background, education, or filmmaking techniques inspired or shaped the work. You could explore why the director was drawn to the story. For instance, are there any parallels between a particular character's life and the director's life?

Forming a Thesis

Ask your question and find answers in the work or other related materials. Then you can create a thesis. The thesis is the key point in your critique. It is your argument about the work based on the tenets, or beliefs, of the theory you are using. For example, if you are using auteur theory to ask how the director's life inspired the work, your thesis could be worded as follows: Director Teng Xiong, raised in refugee camps in southeast Asia, drew upon her experiences to direct the movie *No Home for Me.*

> How to Make
> a Thesis Statement
>
> In a critique, a thesis statement typically appears at the end of the introductory paragraph. It is usually only one sentence long and states the author's main idea.

Providing Evidence

Once you have formed a thesis, you must provide evidence to support it. Evidence might take the form of examples and quotations from the work itself—such as dialogue from a film. Articles about the movie or personal interviews with the director might also support your ideas. You may wish to address what other critics have written about the work. Quotes from these individuals may help support your claim. If you find any quotes or examples that contradict your thesis, you will need to create an argument against them. For instance: <u>Many critics have pointed to the heroine of *No Home for Me* as a powerless victim of circumstances. However, through her dialogue and strong actions, she is clearly depicted as someone who seeks to shape her own future.</u>

> ### How to Support a Thesis Statement
>
> A critique should include several arguments. Arguments support a thesis claim. An argument is one or two sentences long and is supported by evidence from the work being discussed.
>
> Organize the arguments into paragraphs. These paragraphs make up the body of the critique.

In This Book

In this book, you will read overviews of famous movies by director Spike Lee, each followed by a critique. Each critique will use one theory and apply it to one work. Critical thinking sections will give you a chance to consider other theses and questions about the work. Did you agree with the author's application of the theory? What other questions are raised by the thesis and its arguments? You can also find out what other critics think about each particular film. Then, in the You Critique It section in the final pages of this book, you will have an opportunity to create your own critique.

Look for the Guides

Throughout the chapters that analyze the works, thesis statements have been highlighted. The box next to the thesis helps explain what questions are being raised about the work. Supporting arguments have been underlined. The boxes next to the arguments help explain how these points support the thesis. Look for these guides throughout each critique.

Essential Critiques

Spike Lee on the set of *Get on the Bus* (1996)

2

A Closer Look at Spike Lee

Spike Lee was born Shelton Jackson Lee on March 20, 1957, in Atlanta, Georgia. He was the first child of Bill and Jacquelyn Lee. His father loved jazz music, which he composed and played professionally on the bass. His mother was a teacher. In 1959, the Lees moved to Chicago, Illinois. After a few months, they moved to New York City and settled in Brooklyn. There, the family grew to include four more children.

Shelton was a small boy. He was bookish and did well in school. He was also bossy and sometimes tough, which earned him the nickname Spike from his mother. Young Spike enjoyed sports and dreamed about playing professional basketball.

The Lees were a close-knit family. Bill and Jacquelyn instilled in their children a sense of pride in their African-American heritage and a love of the arts. This influence would become apparent in Spike's life and work.

The Filmmaker Emerges

After high school, Lee returned to his birthplace. He was the third generation of Lees to attend Atlanta's Morehouse College, a historically black school. He was a successful student. He also wrote for the school newspaper and hosted a radio show on a local jazz station.

During his sophomore year, Lee decided to pursue filmmaking and created his first film, *Last Hustle in Brooklyn*, which he wrote. In 1979, Lee earned a bachelor's degree in mass communications. He then had a short internship at Columbia Pictures in California before returning home to New York City to pursue graduate studies. He had been accepted into New York University's prestigious film program. There, Lee achieved great success with his master's thesis film, *Joe's Bed-Stuy Barbershop: We Cut Heads* (1983), which won a student Academy Award.

Lee graduated from film school in 1982 determined to make films his own way. His thesis film attracted top talent agencies that quickly signed the young filmmaker. But these relationships did little to help him. Two years after he earned his graduate degree, Lee began working on his first professional film, *The Messenger*. Lee ended the project, in part because of issues with the Screen Actors Guild and an inability to afford the pay rates of actors such as Laurence Fishburne.

The following year, Lee directed *She's Gotta Have It*, a screenplay he wrote. He had little funding for the project, which he filmed in only 12 days. He starred in the film as well. *She's Gotta Have It* was released in 1986 to great critical and financial success, and Lee was thrust into the Hollywood spotlight. The film's success prompted Columbia Pictures to fund the young filmmaker approximately $6 million for his next venture.

School Daze (1988) is a musical comedy depicting clashes between fraternity and sorority members of opposing black colleges during homecoming weekend. The movie earned widespread critical acclaim, but some people do not care for the way African Americans are depicted in the film.

Lee was not deterred by the criticism. He continued focusing on the experiences of African Americans. Next, he explored racism in *Do the Right Thing* (1989), which earned him critical praise. In 1990, Lee returned to his musical roots with *Mo' Better Blues*. The film was the first produced by 40 Acres and a Mule Filmworks, Lee's production company. The name refers to Lee's African-American ancestry: when slavery was abolished in the United States in 1865, every freed slave was promised 40 acres and a mule.

The following year saw the release of *Jungle Fever* (1991), which explores interracial relationships and drug use and received favorable reviews. *Malcolm X* (1992) received mixed reviews. Some criticized it for being long and impersonal.

Crooklyn (1994) followed *Malcolm X* with good reviews, but *Clockers* (1995), *Girl 6* (1996), and *Get on the Bus* (1996) were not received as well as previous projects. Lee kept working. Now established as a talented, determined, and productive writer, director, producer, and actor, he continued to make his name in Hollywood with releases that highlighted black America's past and present. In *4 Little Girls* (1997), Lee's first documentary, he examined the 1963 bombings in Birmingham, Alabama, that killed four young African-American girls. The film was nominated for an Academy Award.

Lee released two films in 1998. *He Got Game* explores the negative impact the cultural obsession with basketball stardom can have. *Freak* took Lee in a new direction. The concert film records a one-man performance by John Leguizamo of his autobiographical Broadway hit.

The release of *Summer of Sam* in 1999 saw another change in Lee's work. It traces the impact of a serial killer and a blackout on an Italian-American community in the late 1970s. Many critics wondered how Lee would or could film a "white" cast and "white" story. That same year, the Library of Congress deemed *Do the Right Thing* culturally significant, and the film was added to the National Film Registry.

In 2000, Lee released two films. *The Original Kings of Comedy* is his second concert documentary. *Bamboozled* is a low-budget satire of ways race is commoditized in American culture.

The following year, Lee released *A Huey P. Newton Story*, which tells the story of the founder of the Black Panthers. Lee's next feature film was *25th Hour* (2002). Shot immediately following the attacks of September 11, 2001, it is one of the first Hollywood productions to include footage of Ground Zero.

She Hate Me followed in 2004. Lee's next films were released two years later. The thriller *Inside Man* (2006) was the most financially successful film of Lee's career as of 2010. *When the Levees Broke: A Requiem in Four Acts* (2006) is a documentary of New Orleans, Louisiana, in the aftermath of Hurricane Katrina.

In 2008, Lee released *Miracle at St. Anna*, which centers on the experiences of black soldiers during World War II. The film received mixed critical and commercial reactions.

Determined, Successful, and Devoted

Lee has been a productive and noteworthy filmmaker for more than 25 years. He has become a force behind the scenes and on the set. Lee continually asserts the need to empower black audiences and black artists through attention to the commercial and artistic aspects of filmmaking. His commitment to black filmmaking has led to

Director, writer, producer, and actor Spike Lee

extensive work developing others' careers in the film industry. He has also collaborated with various schools to diversify and develop programs in film studies.

Spike Lee's *Do the Right Thing* addresses racism
in the United States.

3

An Overview of
Do the Right Thing

Spike Lee's *Do the Right Thing* (1989) follows
a number of characters in one Brooklyn
neighborhood on "the hottest day of the year."[1]
Rising temperatures send long-simmering tensions
to a boiling point in violent confrontations at Sal's
Pizzeria, the center of much of the film's action.

Wake Up!

Before the story even begins, a soft saxophone
solo on the sound track abruptly shifts to loud
rap music after the film's title appears. During
the opening credits, the background colors and
the camera's position keep shifting as a woman
energetically throws punches and dances.
Meanwhile, vocalist Chuck D raps about needing to
"make everyone see/so [they] can fight the powers

that be."[2] As the song ends abruptly, the film cuts to the sound of an alarm clock ringing and a close-up of a man's mouth. DJ Señor Love Daddy tells his audience—and the film's viewers—to "Wake up, wake up, wake up!"[3]

The film opens with everyone waking up. Da Mayor, a worn-down elderly man surrounded by empty bottles, rolls out of bed complaining about the heat. Pizza-delivery man Mookie (played by Spike Lee) crouches at his bedside, counting his money. Smiley, a man with physical and mental disabilities, stands in front of a church, waving postcards of Malcolm X and Martin Luther King Jr. Smiley stutters about how we "still have to fight against hate."[4] Sal drives up to his pizza shop with sons Vito and Pino. These details establish a strong sense of individual personalities and community relationships.

Social and Economic Tensions

Hints of community tension emerge in the film's opening scenes. Pino complains that he "detests [the neighborhood] like a sickness."[5] Sal explains how the business is connected to the neighborhood—that he has seen kids grow up eating his pizza.

Sal's sense of belonging is not shared by Pino, who tells his father, "*They* don't want us here."[6] Mookie works at the pizzeria and seems to want to make money by doing as little as possible. Sal becomes annoyed with Mookie but treats him affectionately. Vito and Mookie get along well, but Pino snarls at Mookie every chance he gets, muttering racist comments. Da Mayor enters the pizza shop and asks to earn a little money sweeping. Sal obliges with a smile, but Pino angrily wonders why they hand out welfare. Mookie and Pino argue and they exchange racial barbs.

Da Mayor gets into an argument with Korean grocer Sonny and rants that this "ain't Korea or China or wherever you come from."[7] A group of adolescents, with the agitated Buggin' Out at their center, accost a white bicycle rider as he brushes by and scuffs Buggin's shoes. They tell the man that "this ain't *your* neighborhood."[8] Race and ethnicity become a focal point for many characters' rage. Lee interrupts the story with a montage of characters of different ethnicities standing alone, each shouting racial slurs directly into the camera. The sequence closes with DJ Señor Love Daddy telling everyone to "chill!"[9]

Sal's Wall of Fame

Two events bring community tensions to their peak. Early in the film, Buggin' Out sits down in the pizzeria to eat and stops when he notices pictures of famous Italian Americans everywhere. Agitated, he aggressively asks why Sal "ain't got no brothers on the wall?"[10] Sal responds that it's *his* place. He tells Buggin' Out to get his own place if he wants different pictures. Buggin' declares that he will stage a boycott. Initially, this has little impact—most folks in the community recognize this individual's tendency to overreact. Yet, Buggin's argument relates to the tensions regarding belonging and authority that have been shown throughout the day, and his declaration leads to the film's violent climax.

That evening, neighbor Radio Raheem and Smiley—both angered by their own experiences at Sal's—join Buggin' Out. The three men, with Raheem's radio booming "Fight the Power," enter the pizzeria. They scream that they want black people on that wall. Sal yells back and eventually blurts out a racist slur. The argument escalates until Sal pulls out a baseball bat and smashes the radio. After a brief silence, Raheem leaps at Sal, and a

brawl erupts. Police arrive and break up the fight. They put Raheem in a choke hold, and he falls to the pavement dead.

Mookie, Sal, Vito, and Pino all work at Sal's Pizzeria.

By this point, the entire community seems to have gathered at Sal's. Everyone is stunned. Sal and his sons stand off to the side as the crowd begins to murmur that the three men killed Raheem. Mookie throws a garbage can through the large front window of the pizzeria. The crowd rushes in to ransack and burn down Sal's. As flames shoot higher, Smiley pins his postcard of Malcolm and King to the restaurant's wall of fame.

Coexistence and Conversation

The film closes the next morning with DJ Señor Love Daddy talking to the neighborhood: "Are we gonna live together? Together, are we gonna live?"[11] As he again yells at listeners to wake up, Mookie's eyes snap open. Mookie runs to the ruins of Sal's to get paid. In the final scene, the two men confront each other. Mookie demands his salary, and Sal angrily tosses it at him.

As the two men talk, their anger seems to lessen. It is another day in the neighborhood. The camera pulls away to show the community. Then, two quotations appear. One, from Martin Luther King Jr. challenges the use of violence in even the best cause. Violence destroys all. Next, words from Malcolm X suggest that sometimes violence is a necessary response to bring an end to a bad situation.

Sal and Mookie talk outside the rubble of what was Sal's Pizzeria.

Lee examines racial tensions in *Do the Right Thing*.

4

How to Apply Reception Criticism to *Do the Right Thing*

What Is Reception Criticism?

Reception criticism is one of several theories that can be used to examine an artistic work. Reception criticism focuses on the audience. It explores ways viewers' interpretations shape and complicate the meaning—and impact—of a work. In terms of film, reception criticism argues that viewers are active interpreters of a film. More than simply absorbing and accepting what they see, viewers have to *make sense* of it.

The audience is diverse and complicated; people have different values and habits. Reception theorists try to understand how social identities such as gender or race may influence interpretations. Film critiques should examine *who* is watching, in addition to *how* and *what* they watch.

Applying Reception Criticism to *Do the Right Thing*

Lee has argued that film "may be our most powerful medium."[1] He is a vocal critic of entertainment containing harmful messages and stereotypes. Lee argues that films have an enormous impact on the ways in which we see ourselves and one another. He demands that filmmakers take responsibility for the images they create.

Ironically, at the time of its release, Lee's *Do the Right Thing* (1989) was often criticized for "playing with dynamite."[2] Some thought it put forth dangerous provocation. They argued that its images of racial conflict and violence would reinforce racial division or even cause riots. However, Lee argues through his film that the power of images can and should be the responsibility of critical viewers who do not simply react to images. Lee's film requires his audience to interpret images actively so they will think critically about issues of race in their everyday lives.

Thesis Statement

The thesis statement in this critique is "Lee's film requires his audience to interpret images actively so they will think critically about issues of race in their everyday lives." The thesis answers the following questions: How should we evaluate the potentially powerful impact of film images on the audience? Who is responsible for the meanings and messages of film imagery?

With *Do the Right Thing*, Lee
seeks to arouse the audience into
more active critical viewing from
its first sounds and images. The
first few minutes are exciting,
with loud music, frenetic editing,
strong imagery, and commanding
dialogue. Film critic Victoria
E. Johnston argues that the
opening interplay of different kinds of music and
images "issues a challenge to the classic spectator."[3]
Further, the film's first line of dialogue commands
listeners—in the film and in the audience—to
"Wake up, wake up, wake up!" The movie *forces* a
reaction from the audience.

> **Argument One**
>
> The author is arguing how
> Lee uses editing to challenge
> the audience to view the film
> more actively and critically.
> He explains, "With *Do the
> Right Thing*, Lee seeks to
> arouse the audience into more
> active critical viewing from its
> first sounds and images."

Do the Right Thing also
makes the audience aware of
how images' meanings depend
on their context. One of the
film's central conflicts regards
interpreting the wall of fame in
Sal's Pizzeria. Many of Sal's
customers are African American,
and the pizzeria is in a predominantly African-
American neighborhood. Buggin' is frustrated that

> **Argument Two**
>
> The author is explaining how
> the film challenges viewers
> to be more active in their
> viewing. He argues, "*Do
> the Right Thing* also makes
> the audience aware of how
> images' meanings depend on
> their context."

the wall is a shrine to only white Americans. Sal is annoyed by Buggin's challenge—it is Sal's pizzeria, and the photos reflect his pride and identity. On their own, the images of Italian Americans would not arouse anger. The pictures become provocative in a particular place, with particular viewers.

<u>Images can produce heated reactions, yet *Do the Right Thing* is concerned with examining how and why different people react the way they do.</u> Sal sees nothing but his rights as a business owner, while Buggin' Out sees a disrespectful exclusion of members of the community from this public display. The African-American Buggin' Out raises a challenge that the Italian-American Sal has trouble even seeing. The movie suggests that race changes ways in which viewers interpret images. Yet Buggin', as his name suggests, is not entirely reliable—his racial identity is not the only factor shaping the audience's interpretation of his argument. His individual personality—regardless of race—plays a role as well.

Argument Three

The author is providing examples of ways the film explores how and why people have particular responses and behaviors. He notes, "Images can produce heated reactions, yet *Do the Right Thing* is concerned with examining how and why different people react the way they do."

Context and audience affect interpretation, and Lee addresses both issues through methods beyond characters and story. <u>Do the Right Thing also uses formal techniques, such as camera placement and scene editing, to provoke active viewing.</u> Many of Lee's favorite techniques emphasize ways in which characters respond to images, events, and scenes. When Buggin' Out first sees the wall, the camera repeatedly cuts to his increasingly outraged expression. Such reaction shots are common in film and suggest that the audience interpret the image the same way a character does. But Buggin' Out's reactions are exaggerated and almost comical. Throughout the film, Lee uses camera techniques to make viewers think more critically about what they are seeing.

> **Argument Four**
> The author is providing an example of how Lee's direction challenges viewers to be more active and critical in their viewing. The author explains, "Do the Right Thing also uses formal techniques, such as camera placement and scene editing, to provoke active viewing."

Lee also provokes active viewing by using a shot-reverse shot in a different way. This technique is often used to set up a dialogue. First, the camera frames, or looks at, one person talking. Then, it turns and frames the other person in the conversation as he or she talks. This editing produces the illusion of characters talking to one another rather than acting on the set. But Lee often shoots dialogue with the speaker facing the camera. For instance, when Radio Raheem first enters Sal's with his music booming loudly, Sal stares directly into the camera to tell him to turn it down. Raheem answers while staring into the camera. Lee uses the film to confront the audience: the men yell at the viewers while yelling at each other.

Lee uses another unconventional technique to confront the audience. As the camera zooms in closer and closer on their respective faces, a series of characters scream racial slurs. The montage steps out of the story, making viewers feel that the characters are personally addressing them.

The racial tension depicted throughout the film peaks in its final scenes. Here, viewers again see how images can shape the way we see and act in the real world. When a small boycott group protests Sal's wall of fame as Raheem's music again blares, Sal yells that he will tear up Buggin's "nigger ass."[4] The crowd is enraged. There is no room for interpretation of that hateful word. All of the complexities of the community's relationships

are reduced into the crude image of racial identity: when pushed, all Sal sees is a black man.

Sal's wall of fame includes only Italian Americans.

The violence that ensues is further evidence that what we *see* leads us to certain interpretations, which lead to determined actions. Sal demolishes the radio, Raheem attacks Sal, and the whole room descends into a brawl, all of which leads to Raheem's death by the police. As the now-larger crowd stands stunned, the film returns for the third time in a few minutes to a moment suggesting that violence is inevitable—a necessary outcome of what people have witnessed. As with racial identity, violent acts require no interpretation. Violence speaks for itself and produces some inescapable consequences. Seeing only race provokes a heated racial division, and seeing violence provokes further violence.

The final scenes of Lee's film seem to argue that images—even the somewhat trivial images of the photographs on Sal's wall—can provoke reactions and actions, and "buggin' out" is not the only potential response. But these final stark images of violence do not speak for themselves. They also are subject to interpretation. They call on viewers to make sense of the film rather than simply identify a message or the "good" guys. Mookie's final act of violence solidifies this complexity: Why did he throw the garbage can through the pizzeria's window? What did he accomplish? How should we judge and evaluate that image, that action? The answer is not clear. Repeatedly, Lee's point is that

Argument Five

The author is detailing a final example of how Lee uses *Do the Right Thing* to challenge viewers. He writes, "The final scenes of Lee's film seem to argue that images— even the somewhat trivial images of the photographs on Sal's wall—can provoke reactions and actions, and 'buggin' out' is not the only potential response." The author reiterates the power of imagery and reminds us, as Lee reminds viewers, that we can choose how to interpret and respond.

Lee on the set during the filming of *Do the Right Thing*

figuring out the right thing to do requires critical thinking.

Do the Right Thing closes with one final paradox. A quotation from Martin Luther King Jr. emphasizing the need to resist violence is replaced by a quotation from Malcolm X defending violence. To the very end, *Do the Right Thing* keeps viewers aware of multiple viewpoints—how we think about an issue or an event. Ultimately, those viewpoints are often shaped by what we see. *Do the Right Thing* reminds the audience that seeing is a complex activity. This film has great potential to incite action and to change minds, and Lee argues that the audience must wake up and take responsibility for watching critically. Film has the power to do more than shape viewers' thinking and actions. It can empower viewers to think for themselves. While the film's title demands that we do the right thing, the film itself challenges viewers to do more by asking them to explore what the right thing is.

> **Conclusion**
>
> This final paragraph is the conclusion of the critique. It partially restates the thesis and summarizes the author's arguments, which have been supported with evidence from *Do the Right Thing*. Focusing on reception criticism, the author notes the power of film as a medium and the broader question Lee asks viewers through the film as a whole.

Thinking Critically about *Do the Right Thing*

Now it is your turn to assess the critique.
Consider these questions:

1. The thesis stresses that Lee's film forces viewers
   to actively interpret images to make them think
   critically about issues of race in their everyday
   lives. Do you agree with this argument? Why
   or why not? In what ways might it be important
   that films try to challenge viewers?

2. What was the most interesting argument made
   in the critique? What was the strongest one?
   What was the weakest? Were the points backed
   up with strong evidence from the film? Did the
   arguments support the thesis?

3. One goal of a good conclusion is to prompt
   the reader to explore the topic further, often
   by raising a new, related idea or asking a new
   question. Does this critique do that effectively?
   How else could the author have ended this
   critique?

Other Approaches

What you have just read is one possible way to apply reception criticism to a critique of *Do the Right Thing*. What are some other ways experts have approached it? How else might viewers interpret the film? Using the same evidence as this chapter, some critics come to a very different conclusion.

Following are two alternate approaches, both of which consider the role of race in audience interpretation.

The Film Reinforces Different Beliefs Held by Different Races

In Sal's Pizzeria, we see how racial differences produce radically—even violently—different responses to situations. Many critics have noted that Lee seems to reduce the idea of racial identity to a simplistic truth. The thesis statement for this alternative critique might be: Rather than promoting the responsibility of viewers in the complex work of interpretation, *Do the Right Thing* may reinforce stereotypical beliefs—particularly about race—among audience members from different backgrounds.

The Film Shows That Race Influences Interpretation

Since reception criticism often concentrates less on what is in the film than on viewers' reactions, a critique might set up a survey to ask and analyze how viewers of different racial or ethnic backgrounds read the "responsibility" of various characters in the movie. The thesis for such a critique might be: Lee's film *Do the Right Thing* helps us see how race does indeed change how we interpret what we see.

Lee's 4-hour documentary *When the Levees Broke: A Requiem in Four Acts* deals with the devastation caused by Hurricane Katrina.

Chapter

5

An Overview of
When the Levees Broke: A Requiem in Four Acts

In 2006, Lee created a documentary focused on New Orleans, Louisiana, in the aftermath of Hurricane Katrina, which struck on August 29, 2005. *When the Levees Broke: A Requiem in Four Acts* opens with an aerial shot of New Orleans appearing peaceful. The image quickly changes. As Louis Armstrong sings "Do You Know What It Means to Miss New Orleans?" on the sound track, the film shows houses submerged, wind whipping the water furiously. The film cuts to a tracking shot down a devastated street, where almost all the houses have been reduced to rubble—the song's lyrics take on an ironic, tragic edge. Lee cuts back and forth between black-and-white footage of a busy city street and present-day devastation. These first few minutes are a montage of images from the

city's past and present and a skeptical assessment
of hope for its future. Before the title rolls up the
screen, Lee has begun the requiem.

Act I

The film is presented in four acts. Each one
focuses on certain key themes. At the beginning of
the first act, Lee shows footage from the December
2005 congressional fact-finding hearings about what
went wrong in the response to Hurricane Katrina.
It then cuts back to September 26 and Federal
Emergency Management Agency (FEMA) Director
Michael Brown assuring a reporter the agency had
been "ready for this."[1] Viewers get an illustration
of one key issue (the gap between preparedness and
response) and a key technique (moving back and
forth in time). Throughout the film, news footage
is interspersed with testimonials from residents,
authorities, media personnel, and a host of experts.
Certain key witnesses recur frequently and serve
almost as protagonists.

Act I studies New Orleans in peril. Residents
recall their initial muted response to the impending
hurricane, which was replaced by greater anxieties
as predictions grew more dire and the city mandated

The destruction caused by Hurricane Katrina was massive.

evacuation for the first time. Evacuation proved difficult for thousands of residents who lacked the means to leave on their own and were forced to take refuge in the Superdome. Residents recount the panic and the fear they felt as the hurricane breached one spot in the levee systems protecting the city, which is below sea level, and tore a hole in the roof of the Superdome. But as the storm passes, it appears that New Orleans had dodged the worst impact—until waters in the nearby Lake Pontchartrain surge and burst the levees in other spots, flooding entire neighborhoods and making the city a disaster zone.

Act I begins asking why and how the disaster happened. The catastrophic failures of preparedness stretch far back in time. Many critical reports about the levees were ignored. And the city's significant poverty left many people more susceptible to disaster. The implications of this levee breaching are linked to historical instances where the poor populations of the city—often African American— bore the brunt of storms and disasters. Act I ends with a harrowing account by resident Herbert Freeman, who went to the Superdome with his infirm elderly mother and then watched her die there, her body left under a blanket for four days before buses came to relocate the homeless.

Act II

Act II focuses on the extended failure of response in the days following the levees' breach. No resources or rescuers are truly prepared, leaving inhabitants climbing onto roofs or trying to swim or wade out. Food and water are scarce or nonexistent, even in the Superdome. Events are complicated by looting and violence. Eventually, under military leadership, recovery efforts achieve some stability. But evacuation is still marked by countless frustrations as families are scattered about the country.

Act III

Act III opens with resident Audrey Mason reciting a prayer. But this opening plea for peace and restoration quickly turns to the act's more central emotion—anger—and a growing public outcry. People fiercely criticize the federal government, some seeing racism behind the failures of response. Many residents and experts extend that criticism to a pervasive neglect of—or active attack on—the poor, who are predominantly people of color. Even as people hope for recovery and return, continuing problems in the city and the evacuation seem to shatter such hopes. Resident Phyllis LeBlanc notes that many of her family have been sent elsewhere and that she suffers from post-traumatic stress disorder.

Act IV

Act IV begins with one of New Orleans's trademark funeral parades: horns, shuffling

mourners, and a casket for Katrina. The situation is
bleak, even hopeless. The progress of the parade is
intercut with a resident talking about the irreparable
loss of city landmarks. The film then cuts to Mardi
Gras to illustrate the spirit of the community to keep
fighting. But recovery is continually obstructed.
The investigation into the levees—the "most tragic
failure of a civil engineering system in the history
of the United States"—leads to an Army Corps
of Engineers' report that blames human failure.[2]
However, attempts to seek assistance through
lawsuits and insurance prove as impossible and
ineffective as the recovery itself. Toward the end
of the act, Lee himself jokingly asks an engineer
whether it is safe to move back in. The engineer
says it is not. The film returns to a montage of
witnesses, including Phyllis LeBlanc, who reads
a prose poem: "[O]ut of all of this brokenness,
. . . I am coming back."[3] The film returns to the
act's opening parade. The horns are more rousing
and rhythmic, and the marchers are jumping
and dancing around the mock coffin—it is a
conventional New Orleans funeral: still mourning,
yet with a ray of hope.

Lee's *When the Levees Broke: A Requiem in Four Acts* shares images of Hurricane Katrina's destruction with audiences.

Lee was deeply affected by the destruction in New Orleans. He was moved to create a film that would document the tragedy.

How to Apply Structuralism to
When the Levees Broke: A Requiem in Four Acts

What Is Structuralism?

Another method for analyzing film is
structuralism. This theory focuses on the
relationship between part and whole and often
breaks down a story to analyze its various pieces.
Structuralists believe there is a common, basic
structure that all narratives follow. While all films
are different, they also rely on familiar conventions
and techniques. Structuralism attempts to reveal
the deep structure of the film, which is the smallest
pieces of the work that compose the whole.
Different shots in a film are combined to create the
illusion of a whole.

Many critics argue that this suturing creates
an illusion—a sense of reality—that erases viewer
awareness of the way the film was created.

Wilhelmina
and Terence
Blanchard
are victims
of Hurricane
Katrina.

A structuralist film critique analyzes how films produce that sense of reality by examining how pieces are put together and how suturing is hidden.

Applying Structuralism to *When the Levees Broke: A Requiem in Four Acts*

As a filmmaker, Lee has said he wants people "to see how film and television have historically, from the birth of both mediums, produced and perpetuated distorted images."[1] Lee's 2006 documentary, *When the Levees Broke: A Requiem in Four Acts*, uses news footage, still photographs, and testimony from survivors and experts to provide a seemingly comprehensive account of the days before, during, and after Hurricane Katrina's landfall in New Orleans. The film purposefully complicates the facts with passionate feelings, contradictory interpretations, self-reflexive film techniques, and political critique. The documentary is both the history of Hurricane Katrina and a critical examination of different understandings of the event. *When the Levees Broke* makes viewers aware of editing techniques in order to question what really happened during Hurricane Katrina and how we are—or are not—informed by media images.

In the film, images and story connect to give a sense of a whole history, of the reality of what happened. Lee frequently

Thesis Statement

The thesis statement in this critique is this: "*When the Levees Broke* makes viewers aware of editing techniques in order to question what really happened during Hurricane Katrina and how we are—or are not—informed by media images." The thesis answers the following question: How do the ways in which we see or hear about historical events affect our understanding of such events? Or, more broadly, how do film and television images influence our interpretations of history?

Argument One

The author is beginning his argument about the use of film technique and interpretation. He writes, "In the film, images and story connect to give a sense of a whole history, of the reality of what happened."

relies on conventional filmmaking techniques to make viewers more aware of how films shape our understanding. For instance, as in many documentary films, Lee cuts together accounts from witnesses speaking after the event with images from the event as it was happening. In one example, resident Michael Seelig is shown recounting dirty water bubbling up out of a sewer drain. As Seelig continues to talk, Lee cuts to news footage of waterlogged streets. In voice-over, Seelig describes hearing a clanging down the street, watching manhole covers blow off as water came bursting up. As he talks, the film cuts to a shot from a helicopter that illustrates Seelig's story.

<u>It is important to note that this editing together of testimony to image is artificial.</u> There is no footage of the event Seelig describes, but these other images help to make his story a more powerful history. All films edit together images and sound. Film critic Robert Kolker notes that the "resulting illusion is extraordinary"—film works as

Argument Two

The author is explaining how the film uses editing to show viewers how it affects reality. He argues, "It is important to note that this editing together of testimony to image is artificial." The author will support this point in the rest of the paragraph with evidence from the movie.

a kind of "reality machine" that creates a sense of the truth of what viewers are seeing and hearing.[2] Because documentary films are assumed to be factual, their "illusion of neutrality" can be more powerful.[3]

Even the most sincere and straightforward connection of image to testimony should be seen as a distortion. <u>The way images and a news story are edited can be powerfully persuasive and seem true and real, yet Lee illustrates how limited, biased, and incomplete such views of the real situation can be.</u> In the immediate aftermath of the levees bursting, attention to those trapped by the floodwaters was at times overwhelmed by media reports about looting and violence turning the entire city into chaos. New Orleans Chief of Police Eddie Compass is shown having outbursts in front of reporters. Lee cuts to an interview with historian and city resident Douglas Brinkley, who notes that Compass was a policeman from the streets with a real commitment

> **Argument Three**
> The author is describing how the film explores editing to show viewers how it can influence their understanding of real events. He notes, "The way images and a news story are edited can be powerfully persuasive and seem true and real, yet Lee illustrates how limited, biased, and incomplete such views of the real situation can be."

to the community. Compass shows up at several media conferences, and his accounts of problems in the city become increasingly more horrifying. Lee then cuts immediately to a reporter from the local newspaper, who says that some of what Compass reported simply was not true. Still, Compass's claims fed media reports and led to real consequences. Lee shows this in shots of graffiti promising to shoot looters, an interview of an innocent African-American man who was shot by a white man assuming his guilt, and various survivors talking about dealing with armed vigilantes made anxious about crime by the media accounts. Some reports linked truthful images of looting to exaggerated narratives, and Lee carefully details the impact of such distortions on the already troubled community.

The documentary also carefully and constantly juxtaposes contradictory images and accounts. Compass makes a claim about violence, and a reporter immediately refutes it. Media reports praise rescue efforts in voice-over, but the

---

Argument Four

The author is providing another characteristic of filming that explores the use and effects of suturing. He writes, "The documentary also carefully and constantly juxtaposes contradictory images and accounts."

images show huge crowds of evacuees stranded on expressways. Various interviewees challenge the story provided by the federal government that they did not anticipate the levees breaking, and Lee shows footage from a teleconference between President George W. Bush and local authorities who explicitly warn the president about the levees. In many instances, *When the Levees Broke* creates a counter-history of what *really* happened according to the sutured reality of official media accounts or the government.

<u>*When the Levees Broke* also challenges its own story to force viewers to think for themselves by presenting competing accounts without taking a side.</u> In some instances, the film is more interested in capturing the passion of people's beliefs than in trying to determine who is right. Many residents believe the initial levee break was caused by an explosion, and they express concerns about why someone might have done so. Lee interviews engineer and resident Calvin Mackie to present a scientific refutation and then turns

> **Argument Five**
> The author is explaining how the film pushes viewers to form their own opinions. He writes, "*When the Levees Broke* also challenges its own story to force viewers to think for themselves by presenting competing accounts without taking a side."

again to historian Brinkley, who notes that these communities have "a long history of getting ripped off" by various natural disasters and development goals.[4] Such ambiguity regarding what really happened demands engaged, critical viewers. Lee's film challenges the official histories and criticizes the limits and distortions of the mainstream media.

Lee closes the film with each interviewee speaking her or his name directly to the camera through ornate wooden picture frames held up in front of their faces. Lee's camera is not seeing the world as it is—the camera always sees through a particular frame and is shaped by a particular point of view. *When the Levees Broke* makes a passionate case for understanding and engaging with the real stories of Hurricane Katrina—but, just as purposefully, the film illustrates and enacts a critical investigation of ways in which images frame our understanding of history.

Conclusion

This final paragraph is the conclusion of the critique. It summarizes the author's arguments, which have been supported with evidence from *When the Levees Broke*. Using the theories of structuralism, the author notes how Lee uses various film techniques to keep viewers aware that they are watching a film whose story is being shaped by the filming.

Thinking Critically about *When the Levees Broke: A Requiem in Four Acts*

Now it is your turn to assess the critique. Consider these questions:

1. This author's thesis discusses how *When the Levees Broke* challenges viewers to question how a film's creation process influences our beliefs and interpretations of history. What additional questions might a person ask when considering this critical theory in relation to the film?

2. The author has focused on film editing to make his points. What other elements of production could be used to support the thesis? How might those elements be ineffective in supporting the argument?

3. The author's conclusion claims that film techniques used in *When the Levees Broke* keep viewers aware that they are watching a film whose story is being shaped by the filming. Why might that be important? What social responsibilities do historical documentaries have?

Other Approaches

The essay you just read is one way to apply structuralism to *When the Levees Broke: A Requiem in Four Acts*. While this chapter emphasizes critical reflection on how films shape our understanding of an event, other critiques might zero in on a particular social or formal structure. Following are two alternate approaches. The first examines social structure. The second is a formal analysis that examines structure in terms of how the film is put together.

An Examination of Social Structure

One of the most pertinent factors in the impact of Hurricane Katrina was economic class, a social structure dependent on one's relative wealth. The film illustrates how people from lower economic classes are less able to be heard by the government and the media. Lee's documentary goes out of its way to give voice to the voiceless. The thesis statement for a critique that examines social structure might be: *When the Levees Broke* illustrates how class structures change the way people experience—and are adversely affected by—a disaster.

A Formal Analysis

Another method a structuralist critique might use to examine a film is a formal analysis of how it is put together. Lee's films rely on certain trademark devices, such as the use of a strong sound track and certain camera and editing techniques. The critique would compare this documentary with other films by Lee. The thesis statement for such a critique might be: We cannot prove whether an event was real or made up simply from its representation, because documentaries and fictional films use the same techniques to tell their stories.

Malcolm X, photographed in August 1963, was the subject of Lee's film *Malcolm X*.

An Overview of
Malcolm X

Lee's *Malcolm X* (1992) is an adaptation of
Malcolm X's autobiography. The film opens with a
bright full-screen image of a U.S. flag crosscut with
footage of African-American Rodney King being
beaten by police officers after a high-speed chase. A
speech by Malcolm X plays in voice-over, charging
that a black person in the United States is not truly
allowed to be an American. The opening evokes
a central theme of Malcolm X's life and message:
African Americans have been and are ruthlessly
oppressed by a racist American culture and need to
define and develop their own separate identity.

Becoming "Red"

The story begins with Malcolm Little in a
Boston, Massachusetts, barbershop. His friend

Shorty (played by Lee) is applying a hair-straightening concoction that burns Malcolm's scalp. Malcolm runs to the sink to wash it out. The camera tracks from a close-up on Malcolm to a mirror, showing his now-straightened hair, which has also become red. He smiles, saying, "Looks white, don't it?"[1] Next, Shorty and Malcolm strut down the street in flashy suits and hats. The camera freezes on a close-up of Malcolm's smiling face, and a voice-over notes that when his mother was pregnant with him, the Ku Klux Klan surrounded his house.

The film moves back and forth in time, showing how the brutality affecting Malcolm's family history is internalized through his transformation into "Red" the gangster. Although restricted by the racist society, Red constructs his identity in explicit relationship to American ideals: a "white" hairstyle, a desire for flashy clothes and money, a shame in his relationship with black women, and a lust for white women. Red adopts a life of crime and becomes increasingly violent and self-destructive. He takes drugs and risks, is run out of New York City, and forms a gang in Boston. But Red's life changes after he is arrested and sent to prison.

Jailed with a maximum sentence, Red's rage shapes his sense of self. He is dragged into solitary confinement, where he chants that they won't break him. Fellow inmate Baines challenges Red, arguing that he has always been trapped by the white man's vision of what a black man can be. Baines asks, "Who are *you?*"[2] Here, Red is introduced to the Nation of Islam and remakes himself again.

Becoming Malcolm X

Malcolm begins reading and writing constantly. The Nation of Islam preaches a counter-history of black nations driven down by white aggression, and Baines urges Malcolm to find himself—to find his own meaningful history. Malcolm rejects the slave legacy of his last name and becomes a Muslim. He vows to tell the truth straight to the face of the white man. He leaves prison as Brother Malcolm and begins preaching to educate others.

Malcolm quickly rises in standing in the local and national community. Initially, he is unswervingly faithful to the message preached by the Nation of Islam's leader, Elijah Muhammad. The film crosscuts between dialogue from Elijah Muhammad and dialogue between Malcolm and

Sister Betty, the woman he will marry. In the next
scene, after a man is unjustly beaten and arrested,
a crowd angrily urges Malcolm to act, not talk.
The camera zeroes in on Malcolm's look of
determination. Marching into the police station and
organizing a protest, activist Malcolm X is born.
He begins building temples and recruiting for the
Nation of Islam. The film's historic images show
how Malcolm's public leadership develops.

But Malcolm's prominence is seen as a threat
to Elijah Muhammad. Muhammad prohibits
Malcolm from speaking in public, but Malcolm
begins to question the moral leadership of the
Nation of Islam. As Malcolm learns of threats
to his and his family's lives, he publicly breaks
from the Nation of Islam. He proclaims the need
to find a new way forward together and reaches
a hand out to the broader black community. This
break from the Nation of Islam is tied to his own
pilgrimage to Mecca. Upon his return, he tells
reporters of the need to reaffirm roots and identity,
for black Americans to undertake a similar "mental
and cultural migration back to Africa" that could
help them define their identities more clearly and
powerfully.[3] This shift in Malcolm's political and

Denzel Washington as Malcolm X portrayed the struggles of finding his true identity while living in a culture that would not accept him because of race.

public identities is not received well by the Nation of Islam or broader forces wanting to preserve the status quo. After increasingly anxious days and weeks, several gunmen assassinate Malcolm.

The film closes with a montage of still photographs of the real Malcolm, as actor Ossie Davis repeats in voice-over the eulogy he gave at Malcolm's funeral. At the close, the film cuts to a classroom, where kids are celebrating Malcolm's birthday—each standing up and, in a series of medium close-ups, yelling directly into the camera, "I'm Malcolm X!"

Essential Critiques

Denzel Washington as Malcolm X

8

How to Apply Identity Criticism to *Malcolm X*

What Is Identity Criticism?

In film and media studies, many critics examine how images shape and influence our identities. Identity criticism seeks to better understand how identity is defined by our relationship with media. Such critiques examine how viewers connect and integrate what they see on screen in the construction of their own identity. Identity theorists examine how those connections shape—and limit—viewers and how watching films becomes a process for defining the self in U.S. culture.

Applying Identity Criticism to *Malcolm X*

Lee's *Malcolm X* (1992) condenses the life and teachings of a prominent African-American leader into a three-hour film. Films boil down biography into a few significant events. The complexity of everyday life becomes a set of familiar plot conventions about how that average person became the title character. These biopics depict individuals whose lives serve as a kind of model or moral lesson about how viewers should live. Lee's film uses these conventions.

Malcolm X is a narrative. Lee also has a larger goal of challenging the way Americans tend to stereotype and limit ideas about black identity. The film's depiction of how Malcolm Little becomes Malcolm X is a conventional illustration of a leader whom viewers might want to emulate, but it is also about finding a genuine black identity in a racist American society. Lee exposes the way identification with dominant values can distort one's sense of self, and the film traces a model for racial identity separated from American racism. However, while the film celebrates Malcolm X's story as a model for defining one's own identity in a racist society, the

> **Thesis Statement**
>
> The thesis statement in this critique is this: "However, while the film celebrates Malcolm X's story as a model for defining one's own identity in a racist society, the cultural context in which the film was released may somewhat undercut that message." The thesis answers this question: How does a film's depiction of a character affect viewers' understanding of their own identity?

cultural context in which the film was released may somewhat undercut that message.

Malcolm X's life illustrates the challenges of finding models for constructing one's self for black people in a predominantly white U.S. society. The idealization of "whiteness" shapes behavior in ways both minor and significant. At three different points in the first half of the film, we see Malcolm straightening his hair, emphasizing how the desire to look "white" is a recurrent motivation for the man, now calling himself "Red." The pain caused by the hair-straightening potion is first noted teasingly. But later, it has a more caustic satire. Red runs around his house to rinse out the burning mixture and finds all the water shut off. He is forced to stick his head in the toilet, a symbolically emphatic image of Lee's distaste for such behavior. Further, as Red pulls up from the toilet, he finds the police there to arrest him.

> **Argument One**
>
> This is the author's first argument: "Malcolm X's life illustrates the challenges of finding models for constructing one's self for black people in a predominantly white U.S. society." Here, the author is beginning to show how Malcolm X's story is a model for defining one's own identity.

The idealization of whiteness is linked to Red's criminal behavior, as well as to his treatment of women. He is ashamed and full of self-doubt, unable to continue an authentic relationship with Laura, who is black, so instead cavorts with Sophia, who is white. The film illustrates how black identification with white images of appearance and desirability leads to self-destructive and socially destructive behavior.

Such identification with whiteness stems from a broader cultural context that continually belittles and degrades black people. Malcolm says he got called "nigger" so often growing up, "I thought it was my name."[1] And Lee shows in a flashback a teacher advising young Malcolm not to dream of being a lawyer but to imagine a good "colored" career. In the opening sequence, right after he straightens his hair, the exuberant Red struts down the street. The camera freezes on his smiling face, as Malcolm notes in voice-over that the Ku Klux Klan surrounded his house when his mother was pregnant with him. The movie cuts back and forth in time to illustrate how the young adult Red, playing gangster in a flashy suit, was shaped by events such as the brutal murder of his father, shown screaming in flashback. These jarring contrasts illustrate the pervasive impact of American racism on black identity. Persistently beaten down, literally and spiritually, Red as an archetypal African-American man is trained by American culture to despise his own racial identity.

Malcolm's first step toward a more authentic identity comes as he recognizes and rejects such racism. He joins up with—and idealizes—West Indian Archie, a gambling boss. Archie almost immediately buys Red a new set of clothes and gives him a gun. Red has a new sense of self, which comes with a new costume and new behaviors. But even this

Argument Three

Here, the author continues to address the topic of identity in terms of culture. He writes, "Persistently beaten down, literally and spiritually, Red as an archetypal African-American man is trained by American culture to despise his own racial identity." The author focuses on the argument in the next paragraph, "Malcolm's first step toward a more authentic identity comes as he recognizes and rejects such racism."

defining of self away from the belittling images of black men available in American culture is still entirely responsive to that racism. Red no longer identifies *with* whiteness, but he still identifies *against* it.

Argument Four

Here, the author explains Lee's use of Malcolm as a character. He writes, "Lee uses Malcolm X's story to argue that authentic black identity should not be defined in relation to whiteness."

Lee uses Malcolm X's story to argue that authentic black identity should not be defined in relation to whiteness. Meaningful self-definition comes only when Red becomes Brother Malcolm while in prison. Malcolm begins reading and writing constantly, learning about the counter-history defined by the Nation of Islam. Through his intense identification with leader Elijah Muhammad and his own reshaped identity as a Muslim, Malcolm is reborn as Malcolm X.

Yet, even this new profound shift to identification with black identity and history is not the complete story. Over the last third of the film, Malcolm moves from acolyte to leader. Lee's film strongly suggests that identification is only part of the process of finding one's own identity. Malcolm's identification with whiteness was wrong, but so ultimately was his identification with Elijah

Lee felt that it was important to tell the story of Malcolm X's life.

Muhammad. Even a more positive identification with black leaders is not enough. The goal is a more authentic conscious identity of one's own. Lee uses Malcolm's life story to show a process of true self-definition, not just a model of one great self.

Ironically, marketing of the film encouraged people to define themselves through purchases and labels rather than looking internally. At the time of the film's release, the United States was gripped

Conclusion

This final paragraph is the conclusion of the critique. It sums up the author's arguments and partially restates the original thesis, which has now been argued and supported with evidence. It also leads the reader to a new idea: How do your actions as a consumer of media possibly contribute to racist stereotypes?

by what Afro-American Studies Professor Henry Louis Gates called "Malcolmania." Although the film sought to engage with "the larger political implications of the meaning of Malcolm X, the man, opportunistic commercial enterprises rushed to market 'X'-brand potato chips" and a great variety of cheap commodities.[2] Various celebrities wore X-affiliated clothing and noted Malcolm in speeches and songs. The man had become a commodity as well as a potent symbol standing for "black identity." Despite the film's constant critique of the dangers and limits of identification, *Malcolm X* became an idea that can shape and influence viewers' identity. Some have argued that his characterization of Malcolm X reflects Lee's own capitalist sensibility. Lee himself marketed the *X* aggressively. To promote the film, he designed a baseball cap that became "the must-have accessory of the year."[3]

Thinking Critically about *Malcolm X*

Now it is your turn to assess the critique.
Consider these questions:

1. This essay's thesis addresses how the film's
    depiction of a character affects viewers'
    understanding of their own identity. What are
    some other ways these questions about film and
    identity could be answered?

2. Now that you have reviewed the proof
    supporting the thesis statement, do you agree
    with it? Why or why not? What about the
    author's argument did you find the most
    convincing?

3. Some critics noted Lee's marketing of the
    film as undercutting the messages of self-
    identification. Do you think the selling of
    Malcolm X undermines or distorts the complex
    message about Malcolm's identity in the film?
    Do you agree with the criticism?

Other Approaches

What you have just read is one way to apply identity criticism to *Malcolm X*. The critique provides one interpretation of how viewers might relate themselves and their identity to *Malcolm X*. The film could be critiqued using the same methodology with different areas of focus. Following are two alternate approaches.

How Film Influences Identity

One prominent way to examine identity in relation to films is to engage, as the preceding chapter does, with issues of identification. Such a critique could focus on how a movie represents characters and how viewers' identities are shaped and influenced by what is on the screen. Many critics applaud the way *Malcolm X* challenges stereotypical views of black masculinity, but others are frustrated—here and with other Lee films—with the way Lee's vision of black identity often relies upon certain sexist depictions of women. The thesis for an essay that focuses on how film influences identity might be: Many argue that Lee's work, including *Malcolm X*, fails to provide complex visions of black female identity, assuming a "male gaze" in its characterizations.

The Auteur Approach

Another way to examine how films interact
with our understanding of identity is to read films
by a particular artist as a reflection of that artist's
life or viewpoint. Auteur theories of identity would
argue that Lee has a trademark style and that some
constant themes emerge from his biography as
well as from his political and aesthetic beliefs. The
thesis statement for a critique that examines the
filmmaker's influence on the biographical subject
might be: *Malcolm X* becomes useful for making
sense of Lee in terms of his psychology and his
artistry as Lee misstates Malcolm X's political
transformations in ways that reflect his own middle-
class background.

Damon Wayans stars as Pierre Delacroix in Lee's film *Bamboozled*.

9

An Overview of
Bamboozled

Bamboozled (2000) opens with African-American
television writer Pierre Delacroix waking up.
His voice in narration recites the definition of
satire—a work in which "human vice or folly is
ridiculed or attacked scornfully."[1] Next, Delacroix
points a finger at the viewers, saying he produces
what "*you* view on your idiot box."[2] This bleak
tragicomedy portrays how the entertainment
industry and American culture continue to
produce racist stereotypes of African Americans.
Bamboozled accuses both the industry and its
patrons of perpetuating racism.

New Millennium Minstrel Show

Arriving late to a meeting, Delacroix is scolded
by his white boss, Thomas Dunwitty. Dunwitty runs

through a list of Delacroix's proposed television programs, all of which have to do with racial and ethnic experience. The white boss dismisses the ideas as "too clean, too antiseptic." Delacroix retorts, "Too white?"[3] Dunwitty argues that nobody wants to see these shows.

Delacroix is so angry over Dunwitty's response that he tells his assistant, Sloan Hopkins, he will create a show so distasteful that the network will be forced to fire him. Grabbing down-and-out street artists Manray and Womack to serve as stars, he pitches a *New Millennium Minstrel Show*.

Delacroix describes a program that revives hateful stereotypes from minstrel shows popular in the nineteenth century. Actors in blackface makeup will shuffle and dance about doing silly routines, entertaining the mostly white audience with their buffoonery. To Delacroix's surprise, Dunwitty is delighted with his idea. Hopkins, Manray, and Womack are shocked. Manray, though, is pleased at a chance to perform and get paid. He climbs on the table to show off his tap dancing.

The show goes into production. Delacroix gathers a staff of young white writers and tells them his idea. He overcomes their initial caution

by reminding them of similar images from sitcoms
popular in their youth in the 1970s. This displays
how the writers' understanding of nonwhite
experience is heavily based on racist TV shows.

Savion Glover as
Manray, *front left*

    Delacroix and Hopkins also begin auditioning
a range of black performers to serve as a house
band for the show. A montage runs through a range
of exaggerated musical stereotypes: a funk band
singing about women being barefoot and pregnant,
a cartoonishly sexist R & B singer, and an angry
and somewhat incoherent gangsta rap group, the
Mau Maus. These scenes illustrate how assumptions
about the "real" African-American experience
are shamefully narrow and how they limit artists'

creativity. The people in charge are almost entirely white, while the performers forced into such stereotypical roles are all African American. The actors are unable to find jobs in an industry still restrictive to nonwhite artists.

Implications of Success

The show airs with many routines from performers Manray and Womack, renamed Mantan and Sleep 'n Eat. These performances and names are re-creations of actual sketches and characters from the minstrel tradition. *Bamboozled* also provides history about putting on blackface makeup and about the various superb African-American performers relegated to such cruel depictions.

The audience is initially uncomfortable but eventually begins to laugh and clap along. The show becomes an enormous success. It sells a ton of show-related merchandise. Delacroix is initially horrified. However, he represses his discomfort and seems to relish the awards and acclaim now coming to him. Hopkins and Womack, on the other hand, grow increasingly distressed, each eventually unable to continue performing.

Bamboozled's third act depicts the difficult decisions faced by African-American artists. It also continues to heap scorn on the consumers who buy not just this patently racist show but also a host of "ghetto" products. These include a line of clothing with bullet holes already included and a malt liquor called "da Bomb." The film is intermittently interrupted with ads for such products. A subplot involves the "political" rap band, the Mau Maus, who sip from their bottles of da Bomb even as they rage about the racism of the show.

The film ends with a shift to a much darker tone. As the television show becomes more successful, the film becomes increasingly hopeless. At the end, the Mau Maus kidnap and assassinate Manray on camera in protest. Next, the rappers are all gunned down by police, except for their one white-skinned member. Sloan Hopkins, furious at Delacroix's irresponsibility, shoots Delacroix in her office. As Delacroix slumps down, his voice returns in narration, inviting us to "tune in next week."[4] The film closes with a lengthy assortment of clips from film and television throughout the twentieth century that illustrate how pervasive the minstrel tradition remains in U.S. culture.

Actors Tommy Davidson and Savion Glover in *Bamboozled*

How to Apply Cultural Studies Criticism to *Bamboozled*

What Is Cultural Studies Criticism?

Cultural studies asserts that a film is more than a work of art—it is also a product made to be sold. Instead of focusing on what happens in a movie, cultural studies criticism examines the forces that shape the making (or production) and the viewing (or consumption) of a work. Cultural studies criticism believes that films powerfully affect society's beliefs and values. Films shape the way we think about ourselves and our world.

The goal in any cultural studies critique is to examine how a film both spreads and resists the dominant values of popular culture. Many critics focus on the forces that shape production: Who controls what movies are made and what messages they transmit? Other critics focus more on the complicated, diverse nature of consumption. They examine how audiences resist and corrupt the values transmitted through the media.

Applying Cultural Studies Criticism to *Bamboozled*

In the minstrel tradition of blackface, white men applied burnt cork or greasepaint to their faces, adopted buffoonish character traits, and shuffled about for the entertainment of a generally white audience. In his 2000 satire *Bamboozled*, writer-director Lee asserts that such stereotypical depictions of "blackness" still thrive in U.S. culture. Lee's film is an ambitious attempt to illustrate the ways the entertainment industry restricts and distorts our understanding of race. Yet, even as Lee attacks the way "blackness" is sold by the entertainment industry, he criticizes those who consume and thus perpetuate racial stereotypes.

Thesis Statement

The thesis statement in this critique is: "Lee's film is an ambitious attempt to illustrate the ways the entertainment industry restricts and distorts our understanding of race. Yet, even as Lee attacks the way 'blackness' is sold by the entertainment industry, he criticizes those who consume and thus perpetuate racial stereotypes." This thesis addresses this question: Who is responsible for the racism in films—filmmakers or viewers? This argument emphasizes the responsibility of viewers.

Lee's film shows how a white-dominated television industry leads to racist portrayals of African Americans on screen. Employees of the television company depicted in the film are mostly white. Delacroix is one of the few African Americans working behind the scenes. This racial imbalance is particularly visible when the writing staff for his satirical minstrel show is entirely white. Lee attributes the lack of good roles for black actors to a lack of black executives. Without diversity, filmmakers are limited as to the kinds of stories they imagine or the kinds of stories they imagine that audiences will want. Delacroix's writing staff, for instance, discusses their fond memories of learning about African Americans through 1970s sitcoms. The film cuts to clips from those shows to illustrate their ridiculous, offensive portrayal of black characters. Even more disturbing, white network executive Thomas Dunwitty imagines that he knows more about black people than Delacroix. Dunwitty rejects the notion

> **Argument One**
>
> Here, the author makes his first point: "Lee's film shows how a white-dominated television industry leads to racist portrayals of African Americans on screen." This point addresses the first part of his thesis, about how Lee attacks the way "blackness" is sold. The author will back up this point with evidence from the movie.

that audiences want to see anything other than the "ghetto" comedies. Lee's film argues that such racist structures inside the media allow only crude stereotypes of blackness to be funded and produced. Diverse realities of African-American life are left out of the picture.

Furthermore, <u>the film shows how African-American performers are often forced into playing roles that degrade black people.</u> A casting call for a house band to be given the offensive name "Alabama Porch Monkeys" brings hundreds of African-American artists starved for work. And the show's star, Manray, overcomes his misgivings about the show's racist depictions of African Americans by noting that at least he will get a chance to do his art. The film cuts to montages about black performers in early film who had to play horrendous stereotypes. These early actors were forced to play the fool if they wanted to be allowed to perform at all.

Argument Two

The author is continuing to show evidence about Lee's criticism of "blackness" in the media. The author's last point addresses filmmakers; this point addresses performers: "The film shows how African-American performers are often forced into playing roles that degrade black people."

At the same time, Lee shows that contemporary black artists are not powerless—they have come a long way since the days of those early performers. <u>Though the film sympathizes with the plight of black artists in a white-dominated industry, it also shows that black artists still have a responsibility to resist racist representations.</u> Initially, Delacroix intends for the show to be too outrageous to air. Once it is approved, however, he begins to imagine it as a satire. Then, when Dunwitty takes creative control and makes it simply racist, Delacroix seems to go along with the decision. Success matters to him, and he defends the show to protesters and accepts awards. In contrast, Delacroix's assistant, Sloan Hopkins, and performer Womack leave the show in protest. *Bamboozled* argues that modern artists need to take some responsibility for the representations they present.

At the same time, Lee makes it clear that the media is not solely to blame for racist imagery.

> **Argument Three**
>
> The author continues to explore how Lee addresses "blackness" in the entertainment industry. This point adds nuance to the previous one: "Though the film sympathizes with the plight of black artists in a white-dominated industry, it also shows that black artists still have a responsibility to resist racist representations."

Argument Four

The author has now turned to the second part of his thesis. He shows how Lee criticizes viewers, as opposed to producers: "Racist representations continue because a willing audience consumes them."

Racist representations continue because a willing audience consumes them. Often, media criticism studies what goes on behind the scenes or on the screen, both of which *Bamboozled* examines. However, a product is powerless if no one purchases it. As Delacroix says directly to the camera, while pointing a finger at the viewers, he gets asked to make only what "*you* view on your idiot box."[1]

Conclusion

This final paragraph is the conclusion of the critique. It sums up the author's arguments and partially restates the thesis. It also leads the reader to consider: How do your actions as a consumer of media contribute to racist stereotypes?

In *Bamboozled*, the selling of this racist ideal depends on a culture where such stereotypes are produced *and* consumed. As in his other films, Lee demands that viewers situate themselves inside this problem. They must reflect on how their own actions perpetuate racist images and beliefs.

Thinking Critically about *Bamboozled*

Now it is your turn to critique the critique. Consider these questions:

1. The thesis stresses that viewers are to blame for perpetuating racist stereotypes in the media. Do you agree? Where does responsibility ultimately lie—with those who make films or those who watch them?

2. What was the most interesting evidence point made? What was the strongest argument? What was the weakest? Did the evidence support the thesis?

3. One goal of a good conclusion is to prompt the reader to explore the topic further, often by raising a new, related idea or asking a new question. Does this critique do that effectively? How else could the author have ended this critique?

Other Approaches

What you have just read is just one possible way to apply a cultural studies approach to a critique of *Bamboozled*. Other experts have approached their critiques differently. Following are two alternate approaches. The first examines the film's commercial success. The second scrutinizes its impact on black identity.

Examining the Film's Commercial Success

Some critics have used *Bamboozled* as a case study that shows the difficulties facing black filmmakers. For example, film historian Andrew Dewaard has studied Lee's career, including the development of his own production studio and work with various marketing endeavors. Dewaard notes that despite many profitable and critically acclaimed successes, "Lee's career has been one struggle after another to secure funding, especially given his penchant for racially charged subject matter."[2] Despite his many successes, Lee continually finds it hard to get films funded. In this instance, his provocative film was barely distributed before fading away. The thesis statement for a critique that examines the film's commercial success might be: Lee's satire of the industry was itself victimized by the industry and by an American audience interested only in entertainment, not challenging art.

The Impact of the Film on Black Identity

Other critics contend that the film itself does just what it satirizes: it sells the idea of black identity. In short, the film and its production history become further evidence for many of the arguments the film is trying to illustrate about how race gets sold—and sold out—in popular culture. The thesis statement for such a critique could be: In positive and negative ways, Lee's work replicates the problems of selling an authentic "blackness" with which the character Delacroix also struggled.

You Critique It

Now that you have learned about several different critical theories and how to apply them to film, are you ready to perform a critique of your own? You have read that this type of evaluation can help you look at movies from a new perspective and make you pay attention to issues you may not have otherwise recognized. So, why not use one of the critical theories profiled in this book to consider a fresh take on your favorite movie?

First, choose a theory and the movie you want to analyze. Remember that the theory is a springboard for asking questions about the work.

Next, write a specific question that relates to the theory you have selected. Then you can form your thesis, which should provide the answer to that question. Your thesis is the most important part of your critique and offers an argument about the work based on the tenets, or beliefs, of the theory you are applying. Recall that the thesis statement typically appears at the very end of the introductory paragraph of your essay. It is usually only one sentence long.

After you have written your thesis, find evidence to back it up. Good places to start are in the work itself or journals or articles that discuss what other people have said about it. Since you are critiquing a movie, you may also want to read about the director's life to get a sense of what factors may have affected the creative process. This can be useful if working within historical or auteur types of criticism.

Depending on which theory you apply you can often find evidence in the movie's language, plot, or character development. You should also explore parts of the movie that seem to disprove your thesis and create an argument against them. As you do this, you might want to address what other critics have written about the movie. Their quotes may help support your claim.

Before you start analyzing a work, think about the different arguments made in this book. Reflect on how evidence supporting the thesis was presented. Did you find that some of the techniques used to back up the arguments were more convincing than others? Try these methods as you prove your thesis in your own critique.

When you are finished writing your critique, read it over carefully. Is your thesis statement understandable? Do the supporting arguments flow logically, with the topic of each paragraph clearly stated? Can you add any information that would present your readers with a stronger argument in favor of your thesis? Were you able to use quotes from the movie, as well as from other critics, to enhance your ideas?

Did you see the work in a new light?

Timeline

1957 — Spike Lee is born in Atlanta, Georgia, on March 20.

1959 — The Lee family moves to Chicago, Illinois, and then, on to New York City.

1992 — Malcolm X is released.

1994 — Crooklyn is released.

1995 — Clockers is released.

1996 — Girl 6 and Get on the Bus are released.

1997 — Lee's first documentary, 4 Little Girls, is released.

1998 — He Got Game is released.

Lee's first concert film, Freak, records a one-man performance by John Leguizamo of his autobiographical Broadway hit.

1999 — Summer of Sam is released.

The Library of Congress deems Do the Right Thing culturally significant; the film is added to the National Film Registry.

1977 Lee writes and directs his first film, *Last Hustle in Brooklyn*, while a sophomore in college.

1986 *She's Gotta Have It* is a breakout success for Lee.

1979 Lee graduates from Morehouse College with a bachelor's degree in mass communications.

1988 Lee releases *School Daze*, his second full-length film.

1989 Lee's third feature film, *Do the Right Thing*, is released.

1982 Lee graduates from New York University with a master's degree in film studies; his thesis film earns a student Academy Award.

1990 *Mo' Better Blues* is released.

1991 *Jungle Fever* is released.

2000 Lee's second concert documentary, *The Original Kings of Comedy*, is released and is quickly followed by *Bamboozled*.

2000 *25th Hour* is released. It is one of the first Hollywood films to reflect the destruction of the World Trade Center.

2004 The satire *She Hate Me* revives criticisms about Lee's sexism.

2006 *Inside Man* becomes the most financially successful film of Lee's career to date.

Lee's documentary of New Orleans in the aftermath of Hurricane Katrina, *When the Levees Broke*, is released.

2008 Lee's World War II film, *Miracle at St. Anna*, is released.

Glossary

biopic
> A biographical movie; a filmed account of a person's life.

consumption
> The process by which film is experienced in all aspects by an audience.

cut
> The term used to signal an edit in a movie, a shift from one camera angle to a new position, or the movement from one location to another.

identification
> The process by which a viewer identifies with actions or characters in a film, which shapes her or his own identity.

montage
> The technique by which the passage of time is conveyed through the rapid succession of shots.

production
> All aspects involved in the creation of films.

reaction shot
> A shot occurring immediately after a specific action, event, or statement of one or more characters responding.

requiem
> An expression of remembrance after a death.

self-reflexive

> A term that comments on the nature of films or filmmaking to call attention to, and critically examine, how the film itself is working.

shot-reverse shot

> A common form of editing in which the camera points in one direction, then the film is cut to show the camera reversed and pointed the other way.

sound track

> All of the sound recorded on a film.

tracking shot

> One piece of film footage with the camera coordinating its motion with the object of its attention, such as following a character as she moves through a crowd.

voice-over

> The narration heard on a sound track during a film.

Bibliography of Works and Criticism

Important Works

She's Gotta Have It, 1986

School Daze, 1988

Do the Right Thing, 1989

Mo' Better Blues, 1990

Jungle Fever, 1991

Malcolm X, 1992

Crooklyn, 1994

Clockers, 1995

Girl 6, 1996

Get on the Bus, 1996

4 Little Girls, 1997

He Got Game, 1998

Freak, 1998

Summer of Sam, 1999

The Original Kings of Comedy, 2000

Bamboozled, 2000

A Huey P. Newton Story, 2001

25th Hour, 2002

Jim Brown: All American, 2002

She Hate Me, 2004

Inside Man, 2006

When the Levees Broke: A Requiem in Four Acts, 2006

Miracle at St. Anna, 2008

Critical Discussions

Klotman, Phyllis R., and Janet K. Cutler. *Struggles for Representation: African American Documentary Film and Video*. Bloomington, IN: Indiana University, 1999.

Kolker, Robert. *Film, Form, and Culture*. 3rd ed. New York: McGraw-Hill, 2006.

Massood, Paula, ed. *The Spike Lee Reader*. Philadelphia, PA: Temple University, 2008.

Resources

Selected Bibliography

Dyson, Michael Eric. *Making Malcolm: The Myth and Meaning of Malcolm X*. New York: Oxford University, 1995.

Fuchs, Cynthia, ed. *Spike Lee Interviews*. Jackson, MS: University of Mississippi Press, 2002.

Guerrero, Ed. *Do the Right Thing*. London: BFI, 2001.

Kolker, Robert. *Film, Form, and Culture*. 3rd ed. New York: McGraw-Hill, 2006.

Further Readings

Abrams, Dennis. *Spike Lee*. New York: Chelsea House, 2008.

Hamlet, Janet D., and Robin R. Means Coleman, ed. *Fight the Power: The Spike Lee Reader*. New York: Peter Lang, 2009.

Lee, Spike, as told to Kaleem Aftab. *Spike Lee: That's My Story and I'm Sticking to It*. New York: Norton, 2005.

Web Sites

To learn more about critiquing the films of Spike Lee, visit ABDO Publishing Company online at **www.abdopublishing.com**. Web sites about the films of Spike Lee are featured on our Book Links page. These links are routinely monitored and updated to provide the most current information available.

For More Information

George Eastman House International Museum of Photography and Film

900 East Avenue, Rochester, NY 14607

585-271-3361

eastmanhouse.org

The George Eastman House preserves all of Spike Lee's films in a public archive.

Tisch School of the Arts, Graduate Film Program

New York University

721 Broadway, 10th Floor, New York, NY 10003

gradfilm.tisch.nyu.edu/page/home.html

This graduate film program offers degrees in filmmaking, producing, and animation and digital arts. Spike Lee graduated from this program.

Source Notes

Chapter 1. Introduction to Critiques
None.

Chapter 2. A Closer Look at Spike Lee
None.

Chapter 3. An Overview of *Do the Right Thing*

1. *Do the Right Thing*. Dir. Spike Lee. 40 Acres & A Mule Filmworks and Universal Pictures, 1989.

2. Ibid.

3. Ibid.

4. Ibid.

5. Ibid.

6. Ibid.

7. Ibid.

8. Ibid.

9. Ibid.

10. Ibid.

11. Ibid.

Chapter 4. How to Apply Reception Criticism to *Do the Right Thing*

1. Spike Lee with Lisa Jones. *Do the Right Thing: A Spike Lee Joint*. New York: Fireside, 1989. 19.

2. Ed Guerrero. *Do the Right Thing*. London: BFI, 2001. 21.

3. Victoria E. Johnston. "Polyphony and Cultural Expression: Interpreting Musical Traditions in *Do the Right Thing*." In *Spike Lee's Do the Right Thing: Cambridge Film Handbooks*. Ed. Mark A. Reid. New York: Cambridge, 1997. 54.

4. Ed Guerrero. *Do the Right Thing*. New York: BFI, 2001. 36.

Chapter 5. An Overview of *When the Levees Broke: A Requiem in Four Acts*

1. *When the Levees Broke: A Requiem in Four Acts*. Dir. Spike Lee. 40 Acres & A Mule Filmworks and Home Box Office, 2006.

2. Ibid.

3. Ibid.

Chapter 6. How to Apply Structuralism to *When the Levees Broke: A Requiem in Four Acts*

1. Gary Crowdus and Dan Georgakas. "Thinking about the Power of Images: An Interview with Spike Lee." *Spike Lee Interviews*. Ed. Cynthia Fuchs. Jackson, MS: University of Mississippi, 2002. 217.

2. Robert Kolker. *Film, Form, and Culture*. 3rd ed. New York: McGraw-Hill, 2006. 22.

3. Ibid. 222.

Source Notes Continued

4. *When the Levees Broke: A Requiem in Four Acts.* Dir. Spike Lee. 40 Acres & A Mule Filmworks and Home Box Office, 2006.

Chapter 7. An Overview of *Malcolm X*

1. *Malcolm X.* Dir. Spike Lee. 40 Acres & A Mule Filmworks and Warner Home Video, 1992.

2. Ibid.

3. Ibid.

Chapter 8. How to Apply Identity Criticism to *Malcolm X*

1. *Malcolm X.* Dir. Spike Lee. 40 Acres & A Mule Filmworks and Warner Home Video, 1992.

2. Anna Everett. "'Spike, Don't Mess Malcolm Up': Courting Controversy and Control in *Malcolm X*." *The Spike Lee Reader.* Ed. Paula J. Massood. Philadelphia, PA: Temple UP, 2008. 91.

Chapter 9. An Overview of *Bamboozled*

1. *Bamboozled*. Dir. Spike Lee. 40 Acres & A Mule Filmworks and New Line Cinema, 2000.

2. Ibid.

3. Ibid.

4. Ibid.

Chapter 10. How to Apply Cultural Studies Criticism to *Bamboozled*

1. *Bamboozled*. Dir. Spike Lee. 40 Acres & A Mule Filmworks and New Line Cinema, 2000.

2. Andrew Dewaard. "Joints and Jams: Spike Lee as Sellebrity Auteur." *Fight the Power: The Spike Lee Reader*. Ed. Janice D. Hamlet and Robin R. Means Coleman. New York: Peter Lang, 2009. 346.

Index

About the Author

Mike Reynolds is an associate professor of English and the associate dean of the College of Liberal Arts at Hamline University in St. Paul, Minnesota. He teaches a variety of courses in American and world literatures, literary and cultural theories, and film studies. His scholarship has investigated fictions of John F. Kennedy's assassination, multicultural teaching strategies, the intersections between science and literature, and filmmakers Spike Lee and the Coen brothers.

Photo Credits

Jennifer Graylock/AP Images, cover; Columbia Pictures/Photofest, 12; Photofest, 19; MCA/Universal Pictures/Photofest, 20, 25, 27, 28, 35, 37; Gene Blevins/Corbis, 42; HBO/Photofest, 45, 49, 52; HBO, Dave Allocca/AP Images, 50, 98 (top); AP Images, 62, 98 (bottom); Warner Bros./Photofest, 67, 68; Gary Hannabarger/Corbis, 75; New Line Cinema/Photofest, 80, 83, 86, 99